a VOICE for the
Caregiver

*Inspiration, Comfort and Emotional Outlet for
Caregivers of Loved Ones with
Alzheimer's Disease*

Jean Wood

Various poems in this book have previously appeared in the following publications: *Hiram College Poetry Review, The Caregivers Rollercoaster*, Loyola University Press; *WomenPsalms*, St. Mary's Press; Art Celebration Program, Long Island Alzheimer's Foundation; *The Quest*, New Hope Books; *Caregivers Newsletter*, American Health Assistance Foundation; Newsletter of the Southwest Florida Alzheimer's Support Network; *The Caregiver*, Family Support Group Newsletter, Duke University Medical Center; *The Alzheimer's Caregiver*, Living Centers of America; Alzheimer's Disease Newsletter, Texas Department of Health; *A.D. Outreach Newsletter*, Alzheimer's Disease Association of Greenville, South Carolina.

Cover and book design by Elizabeth Nason. (www.linkedin.com/elizabeth nason)

Pre-press and finishing work by Colette Schiavone. (www.designbycolette.co)

Foreword

 ean Wood was indeed a "living epistle" – a love letter from God, read by all people. Not just a hearer of God's Word, she was a doer. Her faith was most evident in the very life she lived each day, and especially during the nine years she was a devoted caregiver.

During her late 60s and 70s, Jean cared for her husband, Francis Wood, a hero of World War II. A vibrant, funny and full-of-life newspaper editor, he began showing subtle signs of Alzheimer's disease upon retiring. Once he could no longer recognize his 6 children or his loving and talented wife, despair entered Jean's broken heart. The Lord Jesus Christ became all her hope and strength.

In the depths of her pain, as her husband "faded," Jean found an outlet in poetry, much of which she shared with support groups in NY and southwest Florida. "I never tried to write poetry," she once said. "The Holy Spirit inspired me with the words."

Jean spent the last four years of her life mainly immobilized with Parkinson's disease-like symptoms. Still able to talk, laugh, pray and even sing faintly, she enjoyed many visitors while reclined in her nursing home bed. In these bittersweet years, her family and professional caregivers got the chance to minister to Jean—a "Proverbs 31" woman who had spent her life serving others with Christ-like love.

This second edition of her book is therefore dedicated to her two eldest children, Christopher Wood and Pamela Clare, and to the nurses and staff of Sunny Acres Nursing Home in Chelmsford, MA. Thank you all for your hands and hearts, your loving ministry of "being there" for Jean.

Jean "fought the good fight" of faith in her final years on Earth. Her faith is now sight, and she is with her Savior, the Lord Jesus Christ, in Heaven, where unspeakable joy is hers eternally. It is with that same joy of personally knowing our loving Savior that I can present to you this second edition printing of her collection of poems to bless and minister to the caregiver.

An amazing artist, Jean once created a decorative pin to wear—a tiny booklet with these words in calligraphy: "The fragrance always stays in the hand of the one who gives the rose." As Jean's labors revealed, our sacrifices to care for others will be sweet-smelling offerings to our God when done in His spirit of love.

May these inspired poems encourage you. For the God of All Comfort says, "I will strengthen you and help you; I will uphold you." (Isa. 41:10b)

Wendy Wood
Editor
Long Island, NY, October 2011

To My Husband

Believe, dear, those endearing charms
I once adored, that made you, you
I'll not forget the homage due
The shell I hold now in my arms.

Preface

o presume to speak for caregivers in all their varied circumstances is an awesome assumption. Yet they need a voice, and I feel I have been tempered in my own personal fire, perhaps like Isaiah, the Alzheimer's coal placed on my tongue. Now there's a presumptive statement!

Caregivers of parents and siblings bear their duty bravely. But surely caring for a spouse is most heartrending. And though my poems are written as a woman caring for her husband, readers are free to change the pronoun.

The therapy of poetry is well known. In support groups everywhere people come armed with clippings of verse to share. Why? Because art can reach where non-art fails. All the books of advice to caregivers cannot fill the aching need for emotional expression. Poetry communicates directly to the heart, inspiring its beat with soul-ringing rhyme, sole-prickling rhythm.

I hope my heart touches yours and helps in some small way to lighten your burden and encourage you in your challenge. Comfort is available; one just has to pray.

I love you all—Heroes of the Big "A."

One Day at a Time

Live one day at a time
Then recollect each hour;
Select a single thing of good
And pluck it for a flower.

Like lilies of the field,
Decline to dread tomorrow.
They stand all day in proud array
Not wallowing in sorrow.

"THEREFORE, DO NOT WORRY ABOUT TOMORROW."
MATTHEW 6:34A

Question

Will God some day make whole and sane,
Or give me needles to reknit,
The tangled remnants of your brain
If any thread is left of it?

Or will I some day get revenge,
Against the tyrant with the shears,
That daily snips more vital ends,
And nightly mocks my helpless tears?

My Prison

My prison is a wistful space,
That views the world around.
My tether is as far as he can hear.
The bars are made of duty,
But the key is made of love,
And the sentence is as long as I can bear.

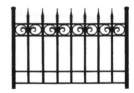

Key

I've learned the key's to think him blind,
For then I don't expect
A quick response of eye and mind,
All normal and correct.

Instead, a patient sympathy
Wells up and I can guide
With cheerful tone and touch (this key
Can seal my tears inside).

But if I somehow had the choice,
To have his former self but blind,
With eager hand and cheering voice,
I'd lock his eyes and free his mind!

Kaleidoscope

The ways of God are prisms
Of renewal and insight.
The darkest cataclysm's
Irridescent with His light!

Back when this evil had its start
My brimful eyes could see,
The pieces of my broken heart
Would pave my way to Thee.

Then fragments formed a circle,
Then a funnel, new and odd,
Walled and overlaid a tunnel
With a sharp focus on God.

Today the mirrored facets
Of my life turn into view.
Upheld by thee, each joy and pain
Glows in a richer hue.

Now pieces fall like thunder,
Light transcending all the rest.
New meanings burst in wonder;
I, no longer blind, am blest.

"I HAVE COME THAT THEY MAY HAVE LIFE, AND HAVE IT
TO THE FULL." JOHN 10:10B

I Am a Statistic

My husband has Alzheimer's.
These four words brand my soul.

We are different.
We are a percentage,
Some of the sum.
You are the difference
That makes the whole.

I am a statistic.

Because of me, you, the rest
Can hope, argue, travel, make love,
Recall the past,
Dine on the present,
Plan the future,
Can be your best.

Don't pity me
I've insights you'll never see.
I know, now, how
To appreciate what you have.
What more can I fear?
When words we exchange make sense
I cheer!

I daily revel in joys past.
To that which was and is good
I hold fast.
Why should I ask
for the sun?
There are still the stars.
My situation a vehicle, traveling,
Travailing
Touching each one.

But don't forget.
Own that you owe me.
I am the statistic
That sets you free!

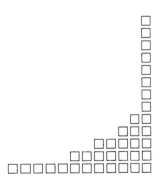

Be Not Dispirited

Be not dispirited.
Open the door!
And flooding in like fragrance on a summer day
Comes comfort, reassurance...
Then, basking in warmth,
Let gratitude radiate in all directions
To depth of earth, fathomless space,
For life and breath,
Eyes and ears.
Tang of taste, smell of sea, satin of baby skin.
Sing of eagles and ants,
Elephants and amoebas.
Sing stars at night!
Sing motes in a sunbeam!
Wrap yourself in delight.
Look! Your hand is on the knob!
The Spirit waits.
Open the door!

"I STAND AT THE DOOR AND KNOCK. IF ANYONE HEARS
MY VOICE AND OPENS THE DOOR, I WILL COME IN AND
EAT WITH HIM, AND HE WITH ME." REVELATION 3:20

Insomnia

O God, turn off my churning thought-stream tight,
And sieze the clapper of th' unhappy bell.
I need the quiet respite of the night—
Need slumber to refill my empty well.
Long thinking cannot drain the cloud of pain.
No ear can hear the tolling of my sorrow.
God only can restrain my teeming brain.
Sleep only gives me grace to face tomorrow.
Set me before the threshold of that door,
I've coped and hoped my long day's deeds could earn.
With grateful sob I'll find again the knob,
My clenched hands unclasp to grasp and turn.

Yet stay awake to pray that God might deem,
To grant the easing of a pleasing dream.

"I WILL LIE DOWN AND SLEEP IN PEACE, FOR YOU
ALONE, O LORD, MAKE ME DWELL IN SAFETY."
PSALM 4:8

A* Wonderland Party

I was the White Rabbit,
And she was Alice, I'd say.

We took our two mad hatters
To a restaurant dinner,
Valentine's Day.

Fragments, phrases...her husband
Made no more sense than mine.
I listened to him—
A new nonsense,
In no way taxing.

And she listened to mine.
How curiously relaxing!
Let's have some wine!

We made up their minds and ordered.
My husband showed the waiter his tie
With tennis racket print three times.

We spread their bread,
And cut their meat,
And sugared their tea.
Then paused to eat.
Camaraderie!

She and I,
With one great thing in common,
Talked of everything else.

We learned about one another,
And each other's
Husbands…then, and when.
Need diminished…
We nearly finished
A carafe!
How good to laugh!

We'll do it again!

*Alzheimer's

Wish

Sometime, somehow, somewhere,
Out in the middle of a desert, maybe,
I'd like to be by myself where no one could hear,
Not even God.

I'd reach down deep into the chasm of the ache
And tug forth
And let fly
A long, loud, agonized, soul-sobbing,
throat-throbbing, crescendoing
Wail . . . .

Then I would return to the world,
Quietly, properly.
Satisfied
That I had confided to myself
How much I miss him!

Alzheimer Eyes

If eyes are op'nings to the soul,
What if the mind is dead?
So much that made the spirit whole
The spirit's home has fled!

The orbs remain, surrounded by
Familiar lash and lid.
They look around; they blink and cry,
But all I loved is hid.

Is each a mirrored light impasse
To mock my proffered kiss?
Or are they clear like window glass
That looks on an abyss?

The Bad Guys

We're the bad guys—
Ones that make them brush their teeth,
Coax them to eat their vegetables,
Cut their fingernails—Ouch!
Pull off a wet shirt—Oof!
Clean their ears—ooo…No!
(Wipe and wipe)
Extract their arms as we buckle their seatbelts.
Then, when we get there
Draw them forth one foot at a time,
Holding their head down so it won't hit the door opening.

We do these uncomfortable things
To make them comfortable,
Physically well.
We wish they could love us,
Because we care about these things
But they can't love us.
We're the bad guys.

Support Group

It's good to meet with friends and ask
Unanswered questions: Why?
Let down your hair, take off your mask
And breathe a common sigh.
Review how to approach a task;
You laugh so you don't cry.

For only those in your same boat,
May know of something new.
You listen, tell, you cheer, you quote,
And lend a shoulder to.
And sometimes, someone strikes a note,
That helps you muddle through.

"PLANS FAIL FOR LACK OF COUNSEL,
BUT WITH MANY ADVISORS THEY SUCCEED."
PROVERBS 15:22

Exasperation

The mindless demon taking over
Stubborn as a mule,
Does all he can to get your goat
And make you lose your cool.

But you show him you know it's HE.
Your love is not that way.
This mood will pass, just fill your mind
With what went right today.

Don't blame your love, blame the disease,
For everything that's wrong.
And pound that devil to his knees
With humor and a song!

"If God is for us, who can be against us?"
Romans 8:31b

Prayer

God help me lift his mood.
God keep me calm and kind.
To everything not right and good,
God help to make me blind.

Not with an actor's art,
But let thy steady grace
Pour warmth into my heart
Put smiles upon my face.

For every thing I feel
He mirrors back, I find.
So give me words that soothe and heal,
Let love be in my mind.

Loss of Self

Caregivers speak,
Apologetically,
Of their loved ones in the past tense:
"My wife *was* a wonderful woman."
"My father *was* a wonderful man."
Not because they
No longer are,
But because they are no longer
Selves.

Shepherd

I'm the designated shepherd
Of a single, needy sheep.
And although my daily care's not always right,
There's a shepherd watching both of us
Who doesn't need to sleep,
His perfect care is with us day and night.

Hurrah!

A thin spot in the cloud,
Can put a sparkle in my day.
Scant words of perfect sense
That he'll occasionally say —

Like, "What would I do without you?"
As he covers up my hand.
Six words of recognition
Are overwhelming — Grand!

The Golden Years

The golden years are gone for me.
These are the years of lead.
Nor any doctors alchemy
Can change the days ahead.

Come talk to me and calm my fears.
Tell what he was like then.
Let's burnish bright the golden years
And bring them back again!

"On my bed I remember you; I think of you
through the watches of the night. Because you
are my help, I sing in the shadow of your wings."
Psalm 63:6-7

Recurring Dream

Sometimes I dream of how it used to be
Before Alzheimer's plague erased his mind.
How many fans were in his panoply
He was so madcap, capable and kind.

I dream of how I loved it by his side,
When he was "holding forth," he had a knack!
Of making people laugh until they cried.
The whole great scene comes back and back and back!

And then I wake and it's another day,
And though he's warm beside me he won't know
What date it is or what to wear or say,
How close he'll follow everywhere I go!

I tally all his needs and moods and fears,
Remember every deficit and lack,
And how I must keep smiling through my tears,
The whole dread scene comes back and back and back.

My inner eye then opens and I see,
How many times I can be happy for,
How many sighed for dreams have come to be,
The store of treasures waiting at my door.

I shift my thinking to a higher gear,
And get my mind set on a better track.
I let God in my dreams to guide and cheer,
And gratefulness comes back and back and back.

Day Care Center

I wrenched my eyes away
From his accusing stare.
They locked the door behind me,
When I left, and left him there.

I drove an empty car,
The roadway swam ahead.
The cord was cut, I needed time
Away alone they said.

But has it come to this?
Is he one of them, then—
Slow-gaited, aimless, vacant-eyed,
A building that's a pen?

The nurses, friendly, kind—
They used his old nickname.
They called the place a kind of club,
They'd planned some kind of game.

Yet all while I was gone,
I worried how he'd fare.
How could he manage on his own
With strangers standing there?

But when I came he smiled.
Forgotten how to mind,
That I had gone my way alone,
While he had stayed behind.

Your Hand

Your hand holds mine as firmly, dear,
As then, when first we met.
Except I press it to my lips,
Now with my tears is wet.

Is this the hand that once typed words
That scores of eyes would see?
Are these the fingers, dear, that penned
Words meant for only me?

This hand could craft and carve and hone,
And gently smooth and sand.
How many lovely things we own,
Are heirlooms from his hand!

These gentle fingers once could lead
Arousal and surrender.
This palm could weigh a small hand's need
For guidance, firm but tender.

Alas this grasp that's growing cold,
Is from a drowning soul.
But I can warm the hand I hold,
Rememb'ring what was whole.

Pamela Wood Clare

My Bouquet

At night I gather all my flowers
And smell them, one by one.
Their fragrance fills my wakeful hours,
Before the rising sun.

Our children are the larger blooms,
Hybrids of you and me.
Each grandchild is a velvet bud
Whose bloom we've yet to see.

Our friends like blossoms, sprigs and leaves,
Surround the huge bouquet.
My arms now overflow with strength
To greet another day!

"EVERY GOOD AND PERFECT GIFT IS FROM ABOVE,
COMING DOWN FROM THE FATHER." JAMES 1:17

Fate's Lesson

If this plight were not implanted
Where would time find me in lieu?
Taking normalcy for granted?
Squandering life like others do?

Once I fought the trap that caught me,
Without hope, not knowing how.
Help me hone the skill it taught me:
How to find the joy in now!

"No discipline seems pleasant at the time,
but painful. Later on, however, it produces a
harvest of righteousness and peace for those
who have been trained by it." Hebrews 12:11

Here's Pity

He tries hard, but with little left to try with;
My sighs have friends and family to sigh with.

I'm here, with other worlds near as my phone.
I'm near, but in his fog, he's all alone.

Don't pity me, aware of all I see,
Here's pity: he, with nothing there but me.

The Tonic Tree

Keep a vigil in the darkness,
Discipline your mind by day.
Hope that's buried sprouts a challenge:
Breaking through the shroud of clay.

Nourish pleasant thoughts of present,
Hoard the past like vintage wine,
Cultivate new gratitudes, and
Prune self-pity's choking vine.

See, the tree that's growing skyward
Bears a blossom on its bough!
Scorn to mourn its with'ring petals
Harvest good in here and now!

Though the knowledge fruit is bitter,
It bestows a healing spell,
Strength to climb for clearer seeing
How to graft a heaven on hell.

"Hope deferred makes the heart sick,
but a longing fulfilled is a tree of life."
Proverbs 13:12

Uses of Adversity

Though sunshine makes hay dry and sweet,
Moist mushrooms thrive in shade.
If lemons prove too sour to eat,
Stir up some lemonade!

A wounded tree responds
By making valuable burl.
An irritated oyster turns to
Fashioning a pearl!

The more you learn of wonderments,
The more you yearn to know.
The greater challenge life presents,
The greater chance to grow!

"WE ALSO REJOICE IN OUR SUFFERINGS, BECAUSE WE
KNOW THAT SUFFERING PRODUCES PERSEVERANCE;
PERSEVERANCE, CHARACTER; AND CHARACTER, HOPE.
AND HOPE DOES NOT DISAPPOINT US, BECAUSE GOD
HAS POURED OUT HIS LOVE INTO OUR HEARTS BY THE
HOLY SPIRIT." ROMANS 5:3-5

Tightrope

I walk a tightrope with a rod,
And balanced on each end
Are two things given me by
God, To equalize and tend.

On one side is his self-esteem
My aid is on the other,
I want to help but not to seem
To hover like a mother.

His pride is like a faded flag
That limply hangs in tatters
Though some may simply see a rag
I know it's pride that matters.

When he's frustrated, it appears
He knows he's not the same.
He needs an outlet for his fears:
I'll be the one to blame.

It's hard to judge just how much more,
Each day as his needs grow,
To help and try to quit before
He rails at me, "I know."

On days when he has slipped a rung,
And I see things awry,
God help me to restrain my tongue,
Adjust and mollify.

I need a level on my beam,
To keep my hand on track,
So he can beam with self-esteem,
And I can smile right back!

I feel that God holds taut the rope
And will not let me fall;
I cope, perform my role, and hope
To keep him standing tall.

Strength to Give

Help me forebear when he can't hear,
Or simply cannot understand,
My explanations clean and clear
Of what activity's at hand.

I strain to think how it must be,
Within a mind so cruelly cursed,
And how he would take care of me,
If each of our roles were reversed.

I could not bear to have him think
Me difficult to love or please.
I'd try his patience to the brink.
My needs would bring him to his knees!

It's then that I can clearly see,
0 Giver of our length to live,
How good it is that *I* can be,
The one blessed with the strength to give.

"Give thanks to the Lord, for He is good;
His love endures forever."
Psalm 106:1b

Solution

How can I prevent it—the way he is now
From erasing, replacing the way he was then?
I want to remember his charm and his humor,
The great things that made him my man among men.

I'll look at his photos with children, in summers,
On travels, and polish the things that we bought.
I'll talk to old friends about fun times together,
And they will remember good things I'd forgot!

Reflecting

Reflecting what he really needs
Is rarely what I think:
Just help in getting washed and dressed,
A meal or a drink.

To all his grumpy, sullen quirks
My mood must reconcile.
In order to smile back at me.
He needs to see *me* smile!

"A CHEERFUL LOOK BRINGS JOY TO THE HEART."
PROVERBS 15:30A

Fanning the Embers

I daily seek an ember of a coal that's still aglow
That I can cup my hands around and blow and blow and blow.
I break apart the blanket of dead cinders, dull and gray,
The ashes of a bonfire mind already burned away,
Until I find a spark of light, a recognition sign,
A fragment of his former self that I can claim as mine!
Sometimes I tell an incident that happened long ago;
A melody or photograph might make the ember glow.
I know I'll find by evening when I gather thoughts to pray,
The fragile spark I nourished was the bright spot of my day!

Resignation

Resignation's when you've fought and got on top,
No longer waking, sobbing and can't stop.
Resignation's indignation given up,
Surrender and acceptance of a cup.
Resignation is the calm within a storm,
Patience far away above the norm.
Resignation's when there's nothing left to say.
Resignation's what I live with every day.

To Music

How can he remember tunes to hymns and Broadway shows?
Is music such extr'ordinary art?
That there's a healthy line that can bypass a damaged brain,
A sidetrack that's connected to the heart?

God, thank you for this providence, this built-in instrument,
That's left when all else fails, to which I cling.
For we can join in praise and share in softly rendered fun.
Together, he can whistle, I can sing!

"HE WILL REJOICE OVER YOU WITH SINGING."
ZEPHANIAH 3:17B

Alzheimer's Shadow

The shadow of a man sits at my table
The shadow of a man shares half my bed.
This thing that came has gutted good and left me
The shadow of a man who isn't dead.

I know that shadows make the brightness brighter,
Define the edge of every shaft of light.
Without the velvet darkness at the day's end
The stars could not appear so bright and white.

Now, when he laughs it's like a streak of lightning!
I love a spark of how he used to talk!
But O, this thing is daily stealing, stealing,
Like drops of water wear away a rock.

And as I walk my deeply shaded valleys,
The evil thing I fear is always nigh.
But thou art with me, shining in the shadows,
My comfort is thy light that will not die.

"Even though I walk through the valley
of the shadow of death, I will fear no evil,
for you are with me."
Psalm 23:4a

Confidant: Lost, and Found!

Assuring words, adoring hugs—
He once made all things right.
Now while he sleeps I cover up
His useless arms at night.

He always was the one with whom
My inmost thoughts I'd share.
But now my thoughts are all of him,
And he just isn't there!

The blood is coursing through his veins,
His lungs breathe in and out,
But nothing's there—word, touch or stare,
To care what I'm about.

However, windows open up,
For all the doors that close.
Now that God's my best confidant,
Communication flows!

Confronting a catastrophe,
One's views on life revise.
And conq'ring fear, I am assured,
More confident and wise.

"THE LORD CONFIDES IN THOSE WHO FEAR HIM."
PSALM 25:14A

Morning

How precious is this day!
The sun slants on my floor,
Our grandchildren all smile
On my refrigerator door.

The fragrance from my stove,
The love that I must tend,
The Chopin on my radio,
A letter from a friend.

I'll cherish every hour;
Steeled not to glance ahead,
To rue the wretched inbetween
To come before he's dead.

I'll charge my mind with fire,
To daily good distill.
With chin up, I'll not see the path
From here is all downhill.

When sun dissolves in stars,
And at his side I'll lay,
My overflowing heart will cry
How precious was this day!

My Face

What does he see? He looks at me,
With newly querulous eye.
What kind of word is borne by nerve,
To brain that's gone awry?

Are features rude, Picasso-skewed,
Or are they tired and plain?
Is mine the face with still a grace,
He loved when he was sane?

My look is strained, my eyes tear-stained
My mirror makes that clear.
I sing because a song's the thing
'Can make my smile sincere.

I only know I crave the glow,
A stable, good-mood sign.
Don't let his eyes reflect the sighs
I cannot veil from mine.

One Good Thing

The good thing about dementia,
And there is a good thing,
But only one:

The loss of one's mind is a catastrophe
Too terrible to contemplate.

So the first thing that happens
Is the loss of the ability to contemplate.
Your loved one does not know what is happening!

Dementia is its own blessed anesthesia
That numbs understanding.
And for that, be thankful.

The good thing about loss of memory,
And there is a good thing,
But only one:

When you lose patience and are cross,
And speak unkindly (and unjustly,
Because your loved one cannot help whatever happened)

A moment later, your loved one has forgotten
What you said or how you acted.

Loss of memory is like blessed forgiveness
That wipes your slate clean.
And for that, be thankful.

The good thing about despair,
And there is a good thing,
But only one:

Despair, the loss of hope,
After the peak, has a descent
Called resignation.

Nothing can hurt you more,
So nothing more can hurt you.

Despair has its own special peace
That drives out fear.
And for that, be thankful.

"ASK WHERE THE GOOD WAY IS, AND WALK IN IT,
AND YOU WILL FIND REST FOR YOUR SOULS."
JEREMIAH 6:16

Walk Thoughts

I
Don't think
People like seeing
Me leading you around.

We make them uncomfortable.
Remind them of their mortality,
'Twit them about their ingratitude.

They'd rather not see us.
Then they could go on as before.
Without thinking.

I *like* reminding them of their creator—
Spotlighting their unconscious lives.
We are endowed with the power of the stars!

Come, let's take a
Slow walk and
Shake the
World!

"LET YOUR LIGHT SHINE BEFORE MEN,
THAT THEY MAY SEE YOUR GOOD DEEDS AND
PRAISE YOUR FATHER IN HEAVEN."
MATTHEW 5:16

Unspeakable Things

I find myself doing
Things I thought I never could
Unspeakable services for the one I love.

The very personal has become impersonal,
The passionate, dispassionate.

I do what must be done
Striving for good humor and grace.

Leonardo said solving the whole
Is accomplished by breaking it up.
In reverse, the whole has come upon me
In subtle steps
And is not overwhelming.

Nursing is inspired by need.
Helplessness is endearing.
Is God endeared to us by our helplessness?

It is blessed to be
On the giving side
Of the equation.

"I CAN DO EVERYTHING THROUGH HIM
WHO GIVES ME STRENGTH."
PHILIPPIANS 4:13

I am his compass, his anchor,
The rock on which he clings.
I am his beacon, his answers,
His source of vital things,
Like bathing and dressing
And merely keeping warm.
Like feeding and leading
And keeping him from harm.
I am his servant, his certainty,
So insecure his plight,
No wonder that he cannot bear
To lose me from his sight!
I'm his agenda, his schedule,
His calendar of days.
Can I be worthy and faithful
And equal to his ways?
As he grows weaker, less able
And needs me more and more,
Make me more patient and stronger
And wiser than before.
For we are sliding, slow-riding
The downside of a hill.
What memoried treasure,
The pleasure of simply standing still!
What precious laughter and parties
And friends and flying high!
It's quiet after, he only,
And lonely lifeline,
I.

Life

He used to say I was his life
And I'd reply that he was mine.
A team we were, husband and wife
An equal shine and countershine.

Today, though we are both alive,
His light is hooded, flick'ring low.
And though I compensate and strive
I can't restore the double glow.

Today

When time is worsening daily
With a loved one, man or wife,
Today, of all the rest, becomes
The best day of your life.

Time is a gift, your heartbeat's fuel,
A privilege without price,
So seize each moment like a jewel,
It will not pass by twice!

Cold Fact

A funeral at glacial pace
Runs much too long to weep.
Instead, my thoughts on ice I place,
My frozen smile to keep.

"BLESSED ARE THOSE WHO MOURN,
FOR THEY WILL BE COMFORTED."
MATTHEW 5:4

Fanfare

Stand tall!
Breathe deep!
Reminisce a while...

Dry eyes,
Rouge cheeks,
Wear your clothes with style!

Repeat!
Bear up!
Walk the second mile!

Pat back!
Chin up!
You're a hero! Smile!

Take and Give

"Take care," one says as in farewell,
As though one's care could go along
Protect one who departs from wrong
And injury whate're befell.

"Give care's" for the ill, in need,
To nurse and bathe and dress and feed,
To plan and drive, to guide and lead.
Care*givers* are a special breed.

Care*takers* deal with things not live,
Like empty houses, graves and such.
It's really not demanding much,
To watch and maintain things not live.

Care*givers* on the other hand,
Must cope with lives in slow decay
Must stave the grave another day,
Must deal with round-the-clock demand.

Yet when I think of what I take
Of nature, music, all God gives,
To everyone who in Him lives,
I give care freely for his sake.

> "CASTING ALL YOUR CARE ON HIM;
> FOR HE CARES FOR YOU."
> 1 PETER 5:7

Policy

I double all I find in life,
To make up for his lack.
I have to hug him twice as much,
For he can't hug me back.

I cherish every sunset twice,
Each beach and butterfly,
And hold up shyer items close
To focus from each eye.

My former life with him I see
Twofold with love and awe
And savor twice again each
Lovely thing we did or saw.

Oh darling, as your mind is yearly
Halved and halved again,
If only you could share
My multiples of then and when!

Unseen Delights

I cannot see the angels that are watching over me,
However there are many things I know but cannot see:

I cannot see the air that I've been gulping down since birth.
I cannot see the gravity that holds me to the earth.

I cannot see the pull of moon that pulses ocean tides,
Nor see the pow'r, centrifugal, in turns and curves that hides.

I cannot see the lift that buoys an aeroplane in flight,
Nor glimpse the turning of the earth that makes the day and night.

I cannot see the pow'r that sends a compass needle forth,
To seek, unfailing find, a force invisible called "North."

I cannot see the wind that blows the clouds and kites and trees,
Not even when it carries roofs and overflows the seas!

I cannot see the power singing through electric wires,
Nor waves of sound and sight that an antenna rod acquires.

I cannot see the life that's locked inside a humble seed.
I cannot see the impulse that inspires a kindly deed.

Though I cannot see the spirit that enfolds me in its care,
God's unseen holy handiwork surrounds me everywhere,

And faith and comfort, hope and love are very real to me,
But love is still the greatest thing I know but cannot see!

"NOW FAITH IS BEING SURE OF WHAT WE HOPE FOR
AND CERTAIN OF WHAT WE DO NOT SEE."
HEBREWS 11:1

Sensitivity

Like a finely-tuned antenna
My keen consciousness these days,
Sensing mini-recognitions,
Finding puny things to praise.

Like a photographic plate,
Super-sensitive to light,
Every glim'ring sign of sense
Records an instant of delight.

Traits and skills I took for granted,
I appreciate anew,
Wide-alert to tiny triumphs
Of the things he still can do.

At this peak of understanding,
Sensibility on edge,
I review what's meant by "caring";
And renew my solemn pledge:

Though the love that I remember,
Soon must perish, dumb and dark,
I will notice every ember,
I will cherish every spark!

Shells

Empty homes of little creatures
Cast in drifts upon the shore,
Charm us with their hues and features
Captivate us with their lore.

Ravaged minds have no redeeming
Nothing there can cast a spell.
That's why friends avoid us, seeming,
All disdain an empty shell.

Surreal Dream

God made my shoes a kind of skis
And since my path's downhill,
I seem to skim rough places plain,
Caressed as wind and thrill
Exhilarate my progress and
Road signs blur by like days,
And at the foot, while others plod
Negotiate new ways.

"I WILL INSTRUCT YOU AND TEACH YOU
IN THE WAY YOU SHOULD GO."
PSALM 32:8A

Bearing Up

When life was young and simple,
I didn't know my fate,
Would be to garner courage,
And bear up such a weight.

As challenge piles on challenge,
There is a buoyant force,
That builds determination,
And strength to stay the course.

The power that waits my calling,
As close as hand to glove,
Was there from the beginning,
His name is God and Love.

"FROM BIRTH I HAVE RELIED ON YOU."
PSALM 71:6A

The Devil Likes It When You Cry

The devil likes it when you cry;
The Holy Spirit grieves,
Your tears the Father's plans belie:
The Spirit's comfort leaves.

Don't dare to doubt what God's about,
Be still, and watch and pray,
And meaning will break out and shout
Like sunbeams make the day!

"Do not grieve the Holy Spirit of God,
with whom you were sealed for
the day of redemption."
Ephesians 4:30

Expert

With long practice,
I have become expert
About things in which
I had no desire to excel.

(Save one.)

Keeping him dry,
Backing him into car
And dragging him forth.
What pills do not work
For anxiety, restlessness, waking every hour,
(Keeping mascara off my pillow),
Feeding him without spill on front or floor,
Maneuvering clothes on and off
(Unclenching clutches without ripping),
Unterrorizing a shower, shaving,
Getting a toothbrush in his mouth—and out

And, when I feel like crying,
How to make him laugh.

(*That's* the one!)

No Kiss 'Til You Tell Me My Name

There once was a woman who lived on our block;
Her husband had Alzheimer's curse.
She couldn't get out much, but sometimes we'd talk.
I'd not ask, his health would be worse.

She always seemed cheerful and in a good mood,
And one day she told of a game:
She'd tease as she tied on his bib for his food,
"No kiss 'til you tell me my name!"

Her gentle words entered my mind like a blow—
How could a disease somehow maim,
How could a relationship plummet so low?
He couldn't remember her name!

Her husband is gone now and she moved away,
But I'll not forget 'til I die,
The heart-mending lesson she taught me that day!
It's better to laugh than to cry.

I never believed it could happen to me,
That my husband would be the same,
Or that I'd be saying as cheerful as she,
"No kiss 'til you tell me my name."

For only caregivers like she and I,
Assigned a grim path without hope,
Understand why our words must be stolid and wry.
One does what one has to to cope.

And at his last breath when my trial is done,
Shall I softly kindle his flame?
"Here's a kiss anyhow dear, our last bitter fun,
Though you don't know my face nor my name."

To Barbara

Our Marriage

Strong on the seas of matrimony,
Scarred by storms come safely through,
See, the rock on which it flounders
Cannot split the hull in two!

Vows, as ribs, join a keel of oneness;
Love is the mast above the fray.
Flesh is the flame of a steady lighthouse,
Fired by night to shine by day!

High and dry in life's end's ebbtide,
Starboard side in ruin lies,
Still its prow points bravely onward,
Still its pennant proudly flies!

Nursing Home Decision

I dreaded, thought I couldn't bear
This state that's come to be,
For I am here and you are there,
Existing without me.

I could no longer lift your weight
When you fell to the floor.
Long since could you appreciate
That I could not do more.

You'll never know and cannot care,
The lost enormity
Of ticking moments we can't share
Without your memory.

I'm all alone but not my own,
Until you breathe your last,
Suspended like a dangling phone
Waits to hang up the past.

For Ruth

The Comforter

The Comforter's a ready wand
That leads me to rejoice.
I understand His silky hand
I hear
His silent voice.
He opens windows to the past
And shows what joys to borrow.
He knows the ways to turn my gaze
From sorrow to tomorrow.

Mothering

Staring out at the rain,
My mother, in front of the window,
Agitated...
Remembering someone cold and wet.

I place myself
Between her and the pane,
Warm body between her and the memory,
My back blocking her pain.

Then I take one rigid hand, one at a time,
Pull them round and hold them
Together at my waist,
Clasp them atop each other
Feel her warmth at my back.
Who was mother, who was child?

She needed me, caring, shield from the scene
But Oh, I needed her!
The feel of her arms 'round me.
Oh Mother, still and always!
Mother, Mothering,
My need fulfilled
Giving—my role,
Her love returned.

For Dorothy

Coach

God is the one with patience,
When we meet at end of day.
I press the "Rewind" button;
We both watch the day replay.

What things went wrong and which went right?
And how can I improve?
I need His wisdom and insight,
To keep us in the groove.

He helps me armchair quarterback
Inspires new zeal and ardor,
Reveals to me a better tack.
Tomorrow I'll try harder!

"WITH YOUR HELP I CAN ADVANCE AGAINST A TROOP;
WITH MY GOD I CAN SCALE A WALL."
PSALM 18:29

Lifeguard

I'm swimming upstream
Against a downstream current,
And I never liked
Cold water!
But there's always
That Rock
To grab when I'm tired!
And all this effort is
Doing wonders
For my figure and lungs.
I'll probably live
Forever!

"LEAD ME TO THE ROCK THAT IS HIGHER THAN I."
PSALM 61:2B

Husband's Prayer

My helpmeet's now my helpless mate,
And helping's now my endless fate
God help me meet the needs of late
She heaps upon my empty plate!

I loved the meals she would prepare.
She always was the one to care.
I cannot even mend a tear;
How shall I ever fix her hair?

I try to cope but often fail,
I'm like a ship without a sail.
Forgive me if I mope and rail,
I'm angry, sad, inept and male!

For Donald

"CAST YOUR CARES ON THE LORD AND
HE WILL SUSTAIN YOU."
PSALM 55:22A

Dilemma

One door's marked, "Women," one says, "Men,"
Now, what am I to do?
I cannot count on him to wait
Outside until I'm through.
And how he hates to go alone
Into the one marked, "Men!"
With walls and baffles he can't find
His way back out again.
I'll ask an usher or a maid,
To guard us from the crowd,
Then take him in the Ladies' room,
Where men are not allowed!
Too bad he can't appreciate
Our privileged bit of fun,
That other guys must use the "Men's,"
But he's the special one!

Advice to Another Caregiver

Never do when they are sleeping,
Things you can when they're awake.
Never waste free time in weeping,
Use it for your own need's sake.

Have an outlet or a hobby,
Something that you like to do.
You can't be all sad and sobby
When you spend some time on you!

Knit a sweater. Write a letter.
Read a book and have a laugh!
Soon you'll find you're feeling better.
Take a long, hot bubble bath!

Counselors all have agreed you
Need some time that's all your own.
Until they wake up and need you,
Get a buddy on the phone!

Caregivers for life worth living
Need to feel and say and see,
"Though I spend much time in giving
This is what I did for me!"

For Billie

Careful!

As a caregiver, it's not quite that I go around
As though walking on eggs,
But I am less casual about my movements,
For I am more than alone.

Another being depends on me entirely,
And cannot help in any way.
Doesn't know the number nine-one-one,
Doesn't know where the phone is
Or how to pick it up,

Or even how to shout, "Help!"

"You take care of yourself,"
Everyone says.

And with God's help,
I do.

"And my God will meet all your needs
according to His glorious riches
in Christ Jesus."
Philippians 4:19

Widow's Well

I went away today,
And took along my cup
So empty that
It ached and sagged
With need to fill it up.

I visited my well,
And dipped it to the brim,
All old and dear
But fresh and clear
With memories of him.

I raised it to my lips
And drained it down with zest.
With joys gone by
To cheer me, I
Can handle all the rest.

I stayed to drink my fill
And felt my spirit soar.
My yearning fell
And lo, the well
Was full as just before.

I rested 'till the well
Reflected back my smile.
The healing mood
Of gratitude
Washed over me a while.

You're welcome to my well.
Come keep me company.
The one no doubt
To talk about
I'd really like is he.

He'd love to know you'd come,
So smile and lift a toast.
Drink all you please
Of memories,
My husband is the host!

"A defender of widows,
is God in His holy dwelling."
Psalm 68:5b

Our Pledge

"In sickness or in health," we pledged,
Not dreaming of a name
Of sickness that destroys the self
Nor subtly how it came
Between us, tapping, pounding,
Cureless, heartless, widening wedge,
Till leaving me alone to keep
Our unsuspecting pledge.

Acknowledgment

My love's conditional: when he
Is stubborn, mindless, slow.
I cannot hide impatience and reproof.
Yet he can no way help
The dread disease that makes him so.
Forgive me when I'm prideful and aloof!

How unconditional God's love
For us, though flaws be rife,
His reckless goodness showers from above!
Make me compliant, mindful, swift
To own He rules my life.
Fit me to be worthy of such love!

"LOVE IS PATIENT, LOVE IS KIND."
1 CORINTHIANS 13:4A

My Pledge

What does he hear?
My words vanish like frost ghosts in the air.
His mind is like a computer,
Without a "save" command.
Like a tape recorder with no play back.

There are no registered repair places.
This mind had no warranty when
We pledged for better or for worse,
In sickness or in health.
Then I didn't know what the worse sickness would be:
The loss of personhood.
This is not the same man.
What is my pledge worth then,
And to whom?

It is worth all to me.
My honor is my life.
Without honor I am dust on the wind.
I have had his health, his better, his richer.
I pledged to both his mind and body.
Even though his mind is gone,
I will care for his body
"Till death do us part."

What Can I Wear?

There hangs the suit we bought when we
Took trips to other places.
And there's the party frock with all
The buttons, bows and laces.
What shall I wear, and does he care
If I look nice or not?
I'll wear the blue, he always liked
Me in that dress a lot.

Brides wear white to show their joy.
They are the most elect.
Uniforms, police or nurse
Require you show respect.
Widows wear black to show their loss
And people sympathize.
What can I wear to show I care
For one whom sense defies?

I Love You

Three little words
That all of the books
Forget to remind you to say.

Three little words
That help you think why
You do what you do every day.

Three little words,
Because your love's loss
Of recall, you repeat and repeat.

Three little words
Bring comfort and make
Both needing and giving complete.

Three little words
Are what you tell friends
Whenever you try to explain.

Three little words
Make you able to cope
To bear up and never complain.

Lament

There are wars and bombs and killing,
People suffering in the fight,
But O, my love is dying, and I cannot bring him back!

There are people who are homeless
In the windy, frozen night,
But O, my love is dying, and I cannot bring him back!

There are people who are starving
In the desert, cruel and dry,
But O, my love is dying, and I cannot bring him back!

There are calls for help and comfort
And a baby's endless cry,
But O, my love is dying, and I cannot bring him back!

There are floods and storms and earthquakes
And volcanos raining fire,
But O, my love is dying, and I cannot bring him back!

Mine explosions, plane and train wrecks
And disasters dark and dire,
But O, my love is dying, and I cannot bring him back!

There's been suffering by millions
All throughout the untold years,
But O, my love is dying, and I cannot bring him back!

There are days I try, no matter,
I can't stop my futile tears,
For O, my love is dying, and I cannot bring him back!

HIS and his

I cannot let his lacks make me forgetful of His bounty.
I often find his needs make me more mindful of His care.
I'll rise and help him dress, then don the armour of His greatness,
I'll praise Him as he helps me shed his garment of despair.

I'll give the care he needs and then render Him thanksgiving.
The ruin of his mind contrasts His wisdom and His might.
This ugly malady of his can never hide His beauty.
And his death, when it comes, will only manifest His light!

Tangles

My love is slowly dying
Like a river that is drying up
Whose waters can no longer reach the sea.
Like the lifeless shriv'ling branches
Of a limb once reached the sky.
Like rootlets of a dry, uprooted tree.

I know, I've seen the pictures
Of the scans and placques and tangles,
That are mirrored in the faces looking on.
They're examining another
Unexceptional clear case.
Another hapless pawn deflects the dawn.

And they nod as they're confirming
With each other reaffirming,
Diagnosing the autopsy of a head.
The final insult to his brain is
That they cannot ascertain
The name of it 'til after he is dead.

(READ AT DUKE UNIVERSITY MEDICAL
CENTER FAMILY SUPPORT CONFERENCE, 1993)

Diagnostic Test

That day...eight years ago,
"I want you to
Remember

Three things," the doctor said.

"Table." (He touched the table.)
"Airplane." (His upstretched arm flew overhead.)
"And forty-four Park Avenue."

Then we talked about the weather for a minute.

"Now," the doctor said to him,
"Do you remember the three things I asked you to remember?"

(How I ached to prompt him!
Those damnable three things are engraved inside my eyelids.)
But he couldn't remember
Being asked to remember

Anything

Commentary

His bright remarks charmed all he met,
He couldn't be outdone!
He loved to get a laugh from
Clever play-on-words or pun.
Today he has no mine of terms
Or humor alphabet.
Rain on the walk, a thunderstorm!
He simply says, "It's wet."
No stimulus, his wit is like,
A gear that's stuck in park.
When I turn off the light at night
He softly says, "It's dark."
Our bedroom's on the north side
Of the house, so every day,
He wakes, and with a solemn voice
Announces that "It's gray."
The shower is too "hot" or "cold,"
The TV's "loud" or "low."
A new grandchild! I whoop with joy,
Laconic, he says, "Oh."
How much you miss of life dear
That such comment should suffice!
Your loss for me's a mandate
To enjoy it for you twice!

Caregiver's Daily Prayer

Thank you for a peaceful night,
Newborn blush that tints my town;
As the course of each new day,
Slopes inexorably down,
From my chores please lift my eyes,
(With your promise to renew)
To the glories of your skies,
As they fade from black to blue.

"WHERE MORNING DAWNS AND EVENING FADES,
YOU CALL FORTH SONGS OF JOY."
PSALM 65:8B

Children

How casually they bring a smile,
By simply being there
He seeks them out in every crowded place.
Perhaps he knows they will not question
Why he doesn't talk
To get a laugh he makes a funny face!

I marvel how a mind confused
By over-stimuli,
In which all public gatherings abound,
Screens out all lesser things like lights
And noises and adults,
Hones in on the most precious things around!

An exponential dividend:
(We're luckier than most)
Because we had so many of our own,
We've lots of little ones around
To marvel at and boast,
Despite, I mean, because our own have grown.

I love them for their innocence,
Their ignorant, sweet tolerance
Of someone who's no longer in control.
Not jealous how they captivate
His interest, make him grin,
Just thankful they can realize my goal!

Their Dad

It's hard for our children, that look in his eye
That says, I don't know who you are.
I wish when they visit I could find a touchstone
To bring his mind back from afar.

I thank them for letters and tell them he's proud
Of their views and news, as though he'd read it
I tell them I know that he loves them, but Oh,
I know it's not like he had said it.

Son's Lament

My father doesn't know me,
His face is dull and blank.
I wish he knew I need him,
To love and cheer and thank.

I long for his approval,
For things that I have done.
I need someone to tell me
He's glad that I'm his son.

Gallery

I walk him through our gallery,
A little every day,
Our dresser, den, refrigerator,
Some I've tucked away.

Who are those faces looking out
From all those different frames?
All doing things, all smiling so
But what are all their names?

They all are young, some very young
Like only two or three,
Young men and women, boys and girls,
And do some look like me?

This is your oldest daughter,
Ant this your youngest son.
And this one in the bonnet
Is our newest little one.

He won't remember names next day,
No point to have him guess,
But I can pose the questions
So that he can answer, "Yes!"

"CHILDREN'S CHILDREN ARE A CROWN TO THE AGED."
PROVERBS 17:6A

Wandering

Wand'ring is a restless, tireless journey toward the past
To haunts where old familiar habits roam
To havens of calm normalcy where mem'ries last and last,
A futile search for someplace once called "home."

Wand'ring is escaping an accelerating wheel,
Strangeness and confusion all around,
Fleeing dumb frustration and disoriented feel,
From cryptic sights and cacaphoney sound.

Wanderers need someone near who cares and understands,
Soothing words distract and reassure.
And, just in case, some safety measures planned by loving hands
And vigilance to keep them all secure.

Want

I don't want to be more patient.
Don't want only to be kind.
I don't want to be so serious.
I don't want to seem resigned.

I want to be fun to be with.
He was once my better half!
Give me a new lens to see with
What I want's to make him laugh!

Dressing

He pulled his shirt on back about.
His watch is upside down.
One of his socks is inside out.
(He hates to see me frown.)

It doesn't matter hows or whys.
Forget clothes for a while
Reproving chatter, sequence, size
Try my arms 'round for style!

This way we'll fight the cold and bad,
Protect ourselves from harm
We'll spread the shreds of what we had,
And keep each other warm!

Death Is a Waste

Death is a waste,
But wasteful more,
To slowly die...
A sticking door.

In sudden death
Tears overflow,
And, washing clean,
Leave mem'ries glow

But daily dying
Is a drain
Of tears and care
And heart and brain.

Till when at last
The door can close.
Naught's left of tears
Nor cares nor woes.

Scarlet Letter

The scarlet A abroad today
Is not a mark of shame.
It is a curse with no known cause.
It has an ugly name.

It cruelly strikes a man or wife,
A father or a mother.
And ev'rywhere it strikes it leaves
A shadow on another.

It doesn't kill the body
With a shocking, painful force
But slowly drains the loved one's brain
On its unholy course.

A double curse is on the one
On whom the shadow falls
To watch a personhood melt down
Within its fragile walls.

O scientists and researchers
Of all the worldly nations,
We plead: Erase the scarlet A
For future generations!

Reading

As if to prove that he still can,
He reads aloud short lines.
Like labels on a box of food,
Store names and roadside signs.

But reading sentences or paragraphs
Or books requires a brain
With memory for the lines before
Which he cannot sustain.

I once was quite discomforted—
His watching while I read,
But now he likes to hold my hand
As I read late in bed.

While my mind races far away
On pillows up above,
Our fingers warm each other
Communicating love.

Panic

I dreamed I lost you in a crowd
While we were at a store.
Some silly, crazy trinket caught my eye.
I looked around and you were gone
But which way did you go?
Oh why, why did I ever stop to buy?

I called your name in panic
And asked around the crowd.
I started out in one direction, then,
What if you'd gone the other way?
Oh who can help me look?
I called your name out louder and again!

Then I remembered in my dream,
I didn't need to fear.
You had your bracelet and were found before.
Some people and an officer
Were waiting when I came,
And you had never even left the store!

To Emily

If hope's a thing with feathers,
Why can't I see its face?
I want to feel its silken back,
And sense its warmth and grace

If hope sings ever onward,
Why can't I hear its song?
Is it because my heavy heart
Pounds far too loud and long?

I need a stronger pinion
To lift my leaden soul,
An everlasting buoyance
To make my spirit whole.

(REFERRING TO EMILY DICKINSON'S "HOPE IS THE
THING WITH FEATHERS THAT PERCHES IN THE SOUL")

A Closer Walk

Why me? Why he? I ask of Thee
With sad, ungrateful pout.
I, wistful, watch how others talk
And carefree walk about.

Each time I question things, the answer
Speeds on wings more free.
The Spirit leads; his star recedes,
And leaves just me and Thee!

"For I know the plans I have for you," declares
the Lord, "plans to prosper you and not to
harm you, plans to give you hope and a future."
Jeremiah 29:11

The Great Caregiver

When I try to get my husband's attention,
To make him hear what I'm saying,
I must feel a bit like God
When He presents something fine
Like a sunset, or an ocean or a mountain,
A blooming flower or a perfect shell,
Or something nice that happens...

And we go on our way,
Not noticing, not appreciating,
Not remembering the Creator.
Not thanking Him,
For the abandon of His abundance.

God is the Great Caregiver
He has been since our birth.
How He must have loved our delight in things
As children!
Then our loss of appreciation set in
Just like Alzheimer's.

A blindness, a lack of understanding,
A fog of forgetfulness.
We who do not have Alzheimer's,
What is our excuse
For not using our minds for
Appreciation of His world?

"FOR SINCE THE CREATION OF THE WORLD GOD'S
INVISIBLE QUALITIES...HAVE BEEN CLEARLY SEEN, BEING
UNDERSTOOD FROM WHAT HAS BEEN MADE, SO THAT
MEN ARE WITHOUT EXCUSE." ROMANS 1:20

Awakened Mission

His brain's a resource then, to plunder and mine,
To scour it from corners and cram it in mine?
Was his mind a sacrifice for me to see,
Life's value, earth's sweetness, love's meaning and Thee?
I'll charge with the new-doubled strength I've obtained,
Enjoy for him, life, and share insights I've gained.
I pledge to give back the first fruits of my heart,
In service and praise, and today is the start!

Roadrace

There is a road that must be run
And though the path be rough
For every task that must be done,
God gives us strength enough.

There is a race that must be won.
A better life's in view.
Against our lesser selves we run,
And God will lead us through.

"...Let us run with perseverance the race marked
out for us, fixing our eyes on Jesus, the author and
perfecter of our faith." Hebrews 12:1-2

Wrest and Find Rest

Wrest your thoughts from the evil one
Who holds your plight like a magnet,
Drawing your mind to break
Against a hard wall of hopelessness.

Rest your thoughts on God.
His twin infinities:
Of space, and its expanding vastness,
Chocked with hundreds of billions of stars,
Many bigger than our sun.

And the minute,
As molecules
Contain atoms
Atoms, charges
And within, more secrets.

Confess the limits of your mind before His
With thanksgiving for
Universe and mote
And find peace.

"THE ONE WHO IS IN YOU IS GREATER THAN
THE ONE WHO IS IN THE WORLD."
I JOHN 4:4B

Nightmare

A bad dream while I sleep
Frightful, grotesque or fake,
Could never equal horror to
The nightmare when I wake.

I Shall Not List My Troubles

I shall not list my troubles,
Instead I will recite,
Of beauty, fun and what I love
Of everything that's right.

I shall not count my problems,
Instead I shall add up
How friends and times and memories
Still overflow my cup.

Don't detail flaws and defects,
Instead elaborate,
On wonders of the universe
And how your God is great!

"BUT SEEK FIRST HIS KINGDOM AND
HIS RIGHTEOUSNESS, AND ALL THESE THINGS
WILL BE GIVEN TO YOU AS WELL."
MATTHEW 6:33

Childish?

Don't say it's like caring for a child.
That simile infuriates me so!

Children are not disinterested,
Stubborn, slow, grumpy, contrary.
Occupied with bathroom, warmth, anxiety,
Unable to learn.

Children learn something new every day, hour, minute.
Little brain cells grow furiously as they sleep.
Each new lesson, a delight,
Each success a triumph,
To be shared with others and savored.

The Alzheimer brain is dying.
Abilities lessen each day.
There is little delight.
Sharing is pain.
Laughter is to hide tears.
Sadness, omnipresent.

However, one thing captures interest to the end:
(However jaded, however dulled,)
A child!

Patience

Patience is not covering up of impatience,
Like a lid covers the bubbling pops of a cooking pot,
Letting pressure build up.

Patience is not the holding back of impatience,
Like a dam holds back the weight and flow of a river
And makes a lake.

Patience is not a mask,
Like an actor pretending to be someone else,
Playing a role, under control, for a while.

Isaac Watt knew steam lifts lids!

Dams burst and let deluge thunder!

Masks cannot hide tone of voice!
("Beware the temper of a patient man," said Thomas Aquinas.)

Patience is love, longsuffering kindness,
Born of memory, cooled by loyalty, soothed by gratitude.

Mercy, that like Shakespeare's rain, not strained, blesses twice.
If I would bless, be blessed,

Damn! Oh, I would be patient!

"IT IS BETTER TO BE PATIENT THAN POWERFUL;
IT IS BETTER TO HAVE SELF-CONTROL
THAN TO CONQUER A CITY."
PROVERBS 16:32

This Mind

This mind so mere, so little left,
That sparkled like a pool,
Is now too poor, too sore bereft
To qualify a fool.

The power of this dread disease
Of mountain makes a crater.
God who creates the stars and seas
The Comforter is greater.

Be Not Proud

Be not proud! If you or friends
Have faculties intact.
No one is wise to earn escape
From Alzheimer's subtract.

Advanced in age, but still alert?
The proper attitude
Is sympathy for those who aren't
And simple gratitude!

Sing No Sad Songs

Sing no sad songs for me.
For I have known the heights,
And walked beside a shining sea,
And under starry nights,
With such a love that angels bent
To envy such as we,
And ponder what an earth love meant.
Sing no sad songs for me!

Sing praise to mighty God,
For I have known His light,
And felt His tender chastening rod
In bitter depth of night,
And walked His way of comforting,
That other feet have trod,
Sing no sad songs for me, therefore
Sing praise to mighty God!

"SHOUT WITH JOY TO GOD, ALL THE EARTH."
PSALM 66:1

Which Was Worse?

After it was all over
I went for a trim.
My hair was so neglected…

(I knew that her husband had dropped dead
Three years before.)

We talked about how wonderful it was
To have been married
To a man everyone loved.

Also about her shock and how she was
only now beginning to cope.

Which was worse?

(I'd had plenty of time to grieve
and plan ahead.)

I think this was her way of giving her opinion:
"I had a customer.
She'd had 'it' for a while.
I was helping her under the dryer, and she said,

'I know I need to wipe my nose,
But I don't know where it is.'"

To Pat

Unexpected Freedom

The kindest touch of God came
Afterwards when he was gone:
My memories were purified
Of *it* as life went on.
Now when I think of him at all,
He's like he was before.
And when I dream of him, he's tall
And young. I can adore
Once more the love I loved so well,
The mind that once loved me.
I thank you, God, for taking *it*
To make me truly free.

THE LORD GIVES ME "A CROWN OF BEAUTY INSTEAD OF
ASHES, THE OIL OF GLADNESS INSTEAD OF MOURNING,
AND A GARMENT OF PRAISE INSTEAD OF
A SPIRIT OF DESPAIR."
ISAIAH 61:3

My Outlet

Like a piece of varied knitting,
One picks up from time to time,
Little poems at each sitting,
Seem to gather form and rhyme.

Had I more time for composing,
Prob'ly nothing would occur,
But sometimes when he is dozing,
I can give my thoughts a stir.

Then when he is soundly napping,
Comes a period I can steal,
So I plug in my computer,
And I input how I feel.

Herds of words come tumbling, jumbled
So that always it's a shock
How I'm lent a temporary
Grace to make them interlock.

What relief to empty out my thoughts,
And edit for a stint.
Then I press another button,
And I find myself in print!

One holds up a finished mitten
To admire or deplore,
But the cast off words I've written,
Are just outgrown thoughts I wore.

Morning Snow

Waked soundless from heavy sleep,
Myriad descending flakes,
Hurrying to greet the earth,
Tiny crystals, clustered cakes.

Silent, sprinkled miracles,
Crumbling, tumbling, profligate,
Whiting out dark, muddy tracks,
Tasks neglected, broken gate,

Draping pillaged garden rows,
Melding tangled thicket cane,
Soften rocks, depressions fill,
Making rugged places plain.

Layer on layer, the lacy veil,
Like the blessed Lamb, your Son,
Covers, smoothes, erases, cleans,
Things done wrong and things undone.

Mystery love gift, once for all,
Broadcast so each might be,
Owning human bogged stains,
Fit for holy eyes to see.

"ABOVE ALL, LOVE EACH OTHER DEEPLY, BECAUSE LOVE
COVERS OVER A MULTITUDE OF SINS." I PETER 4:8

Dedication

If you admire the verse you heard,
Find comfort in the thoughts you read,
Don't thank me for a single word.
I am a simple hollow reed,
Through which His inspiration drains...
A barren canvas on the land,
Which it miraculously stains,
As He directs my moving hand.
For your words of thanks or praise
I am a humble hearth for fire
On which kind, kindled thoughts can rise
As incense to their rightful sire.

"GOD, MY MAKER, WHO GIVES [ME]
SONGS IN THE NIGHT."
JOB 35:10

Index

Made in the USA
Charleston, SC
30 September 2012